Contemplations

Poetry by Equest'

*To Bill & Ginny —
I hope you enjoy
reading these ---
Best wishes always,
                    Love,
                    Lee & Jean*

Contemplations

Poetry by: Equest[1]

aka: Lee Horsman

The poems, songs, readings, and one stage play contained in the pages of this publication represent my humble efforts to pen classic rhyme schemes as well as free form and some prose.

The lyrics to the songs recorded here will outlive the melodies since only one, *Have You Listened*, has been scored. Unless I record the melodies by singing them onto a sound track, they will be lost when I can no longer sing them.

I hope all who read these will enjoy them and perhaps find some level of inspiration from them.

ISBN—13: 978—1545481929

ISBN—10: 154548192X

Contemplations

Poetry by:

Equest[1] *is dedicated to Dr. Mabel Oiesen*

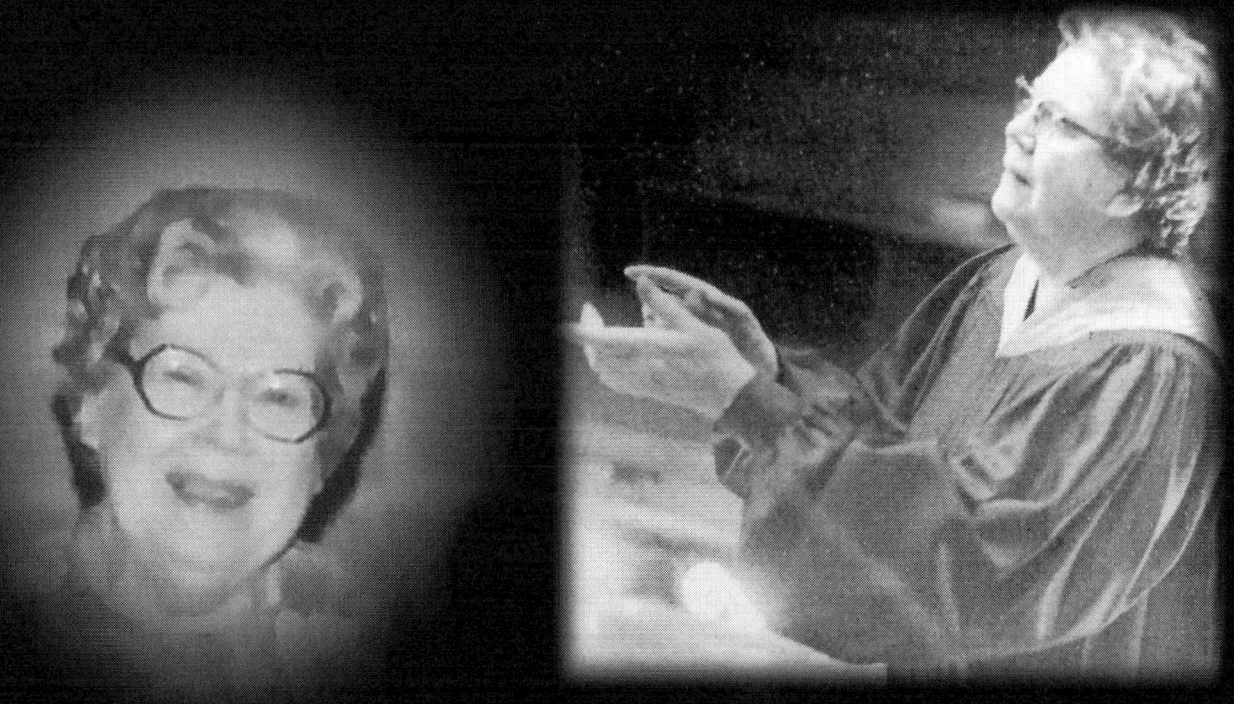

...the greatest artist I've ever known....

Contemplations — Poetry by Equest', is a collection of original writings by Equest', aka: Lee Horsman. A binder containing the originals is archived in the author's filing cabinet.

All publication rights are reserved and copying or publication in whole or any part is strictly prohibited without the written consent of the author, Leroy R. Horsman.

Copyright: 2017

ISBN-13: 978-1545481929

ISBN-10: 154548192X

Table Of Contents

Section I: Random Topics

Page

1. Fowl Remarks
2. People
3. Dad's Generation
4. On The Thames
5. On Sightless Eyes
6. On Drowning
7. On Challenges
8. Iowa
9. I Am My Own Astronaut
10. Old Age vs Youth
11. Getting A Rearing
12. Visual Arts and Music
13. The Senator
14. The Farmer
15. Spoiled Victor
16. Soul Exhumed
17. Somnambulism Attempting
18. Sarcasm Or Sincerity
19. Russian Woman
20. Random Imponderables
21. Paternal Concerns
22. Mother's Face
23. Inevitability
24. The Gunnison
25. De Niggah
26. At Knighting
27. Today's Tomorrow
28. Depression Destroyed: Optimism Qualified

Section II: God In MInd

Page

1. New Life In A Scrub Oak
2. Letter to Dr. McGhee
3. Why War, God?
4. Upon Acceptance
5. Summer Sanctuary
6. I Heard God
7. God's Choicest
8. All For What?
9. A Poem For Dr. Oiesen p1
10. A Poem For Dr. Oiesen p2
11. Letter to Dr. Oiesen

Section III: Songs

Page

1. A Touch Of Tenderness
2. Stillborn
3. Have You Listened?
4. Abandoned
5. Sandy Sea
6. Do You Believe?
7. Cast Your Bread Upon The Water
8. A Cowboy Falls

Section IV: Limited Distribution

1. Passions Expressed While Listening To A Piano Concert On A Stereo Record
2. Soul Of A Child p1
3. Soul Of A Child p2
4. My Trip
5. Spicy
6. I Love My Pharmacy

Total Pieces: 51

Section I

Random Topics

Fowl Remarks

By: Equest'

Talk not in generality,

speak only in specific;

it develops personality

and makes your words signific'.

Don't be like old rhinoceros

with vision all obscured;

but, make your words innocuous

and easily endured.

Why do you let your speech betray you

everywhere you go?

Let "yea" by "yea,"

and "nay" be "nay;"

meaning simply, "yes," or "no!"

The magpie speaks with forked tongue,

the jaybird hollers: "thief!"

The hawk screams, "fight to save our young!"

The dove promises relief.

Both, dove and hawk, propound in flight

all sorts of contradictions.

With birds like these to solve our plight,

how can we make predictions?

By: Equest'

A cloud in the night

    passes over unseen

        and leaves just its mist

            to dampen the green.

The full, pregnant bosom

    of each mother cloud

        gives up her raindrops

            to Earth's greedy crowd.

A shadow of spirit,

    it's gone evermore

        to haunt someone else

            with its moist, pungent spoor.

Mother Cloud and her children

    will again reunite

    to sweep over history

        as a cloud in the night.

Author's note: This may be more aptly titled: ***Revolutions***.

Dad's Generation

By: Equest'

You have to go where the job is,
you have to follow your trade;
you may have to follow the macadam,
or go where the crops will be made.

You may have to follow the crosstie,
or bridge the wide river's flow;
no matter how much you like your place,
you have to go where the jobs go.

You may have to leave your wife at home
to soar over clouds of white;
or walk through the asphalt jungles
to follow the jackhammer's bite.

Your love may be for the country
with its smell of new mown hay;
but, you have to go where the job is,
in city, or desert or bay.

You may find some use for the ocean,
or for the desert's hot sand;
but, you have to go where the job is,
regardless of air, sea or land.

You may find yourself in a business,
or serving mankind through research;
but, you have to go where the job is,
in hospital, bakery or church.

You may be a teacher or lawyer,
or find yourself wrapped up in politics;
you may even wind up a doctor,
or magician with bag full of tricks.

You may entertain folks with your voice,
or become a writer of song;
but, you have to go where the job is,
in order to just get along.

On The Thames

By: Equest'

The cold gray castle by the moor

    bemoans the days of yesteryear

        with creaks and groans of rocky strain

            and ghostly sounds of clanking chain.

The cold gray castle by the moor

    with knightly pride sneers at time;

        its battle banners limp and torn

            still face the wind in limpid scorn.

The cold gray castle by the moor

    has as its precious legacy

        adventure logs of battles fought —

            of maidens fair and Lancelot.

The cold gray castle by the moor

    lets down its ancient oaken jaw

        and stands before you now as then

            just daring you to come on in!

On Sightless Eyes

By Equest'

A single blade of grass

touched my lips

and let me see the lawn

my bare feet wished to pass.

I see the cold unyielding walk

with measured cracks

leading to the house, the steps,

up which I stalk.

Before I knock, I stoop to see

the beauty of the hidden rose

with fingertips and nostrils flared

our generous God has given me.

On Drowning

By Equest'

I cry aloud in grief, despair and loneliness,
    a wretched, tortured loneliness;
        the swamping, suffocating, murky waves
            of loneliness.

A wispy, irresistible darkness
    slowly pervades the conscious thought
        and violent, panic-fraught fight
            for life.

Before my sightless eyes, like psychedelic sadism
    flash vistas of short life's events
        in living, brilliant, blended wheels
            of scarlets, yellows, and oranges.

Oh God of Life, now God of Death,
    where is your hand I've trampled on
        to lift me from this damp and clammy pit
            of hell?

No, no, no, no—just one more breath,
    please, dear God, just one more without
        the cruel and unrelenting brine
            invading choked and gasping mouth and lung.

Oh sweet peace and soothing salve of death,
    why did I fight thee?
In chains of drowning,
    in depths of darkness, I'm released
        to freedoms and bathed in hues
            no mortal ever savored.

Captor now is captive —
life in death is freedom more.

Drowning brought me sweet relief.

On Challenges

By: Equest'

Jagged crag of Himalaya
  reaches up — slashing
    unprotected sky ...
      wresting from its vaporous glands
      tears of rain and snow.

While far below this craggy spire,
  the sea swells and foams
    in undulating fields of wave on wave,
      finding rest upon the sand
      of isle or cay.

And yet, the sea is broken too;
  she yields a briny tear to cliff
    and rocky, jagged jetty —
      made by man to save himself
        from one much greater —
        Neptune.

Across the barren, wasted space
  of cactus, mirage and blinding sand,
    the desert's edge bends
      its bony finger in a beckoning call
        to come on over and —
        — "Pit your wits against mine."

Oh, deceiving woman of desert temptation;
  how many have you claimed in your inferno,
    your furnace, second only to eternal hell
      in draining from the souls of men
        their pride and will to live?

Oh, pathless ocean,
  where are the sailors,
    seduced by Siren,
      to gaze upon the other side —
        — who never saw this side
        again?

And you, you lofty height
  of unmarked crevasse and glacier slick;
    how can you fool a man into thinking
      you lead the way to Heaven's door;
      then mar his life
        by turning into
        Babel?

Lofty peak,
  scorching desert,
    fathoms deeper than the very soul of man
      have given us their challenges
        and claimed the lives of many
        an unfortunate dreamer.

But, dream on
  my foolish, brave young man!
    for what is life
      if not but for adventure's sake?
        What will you give your life to
        if not a lark or quest
          with highest stakes?

Avoid the difficult and trying place;
  answer roll among the call
    for those who leave life weaker
      than when they came —
        nothing ventured,
        nothing gained.

 Iowa

By: Equest

What once was grassy rolling plain,
is now a city, farm or road;
the grassy hills cannot regain
a face God had on them bestowed.

Snow once trampled by buffalo herd;
miles of waist-high prairie grass;
Indian, antelope, wildlife endured
everything but the plow's first pass.

Now corn grows high on feathered stalk
from black earth ridges silty sown;
in these forests farmers talk
among the tassels sighing—blown.

Deaf ears strain to hear the chat;
dew dries out on broadsword leaves;
the ditch—a home for ol' muskrat,
a shovel oft' his home receives.

Callused knees from 'berry straw;
bluebells on a grassy knoll;
mem'ries of the lovely law
of nature's wealth and farmers' toll.

Black earth turned gives up its smell
of centuries micro-filmed and stored;
of all those years what can we tell?
Our harvest is those years' reward.

I Am My Own Astronaut

By Equest'

Deepest depths of darkest blue,
a midnight shade of blackest hue,
lies beyond where we can go
and calls to me.

What is there there
beyond the sphere
of space that we now know—
among the stars where we can't go?

I'll travel there upon a beam
of light which I must call my dream,
that knows no bonds or prison bars
to keep me from the land of stars.

No rocket ship shall ever go
to lands of which I only know;
for scientists shall never find
the star I visit in my mind.

Old Age vs Youth

By: Equest'

Oh, the summer's long hot days
    brings to life those old clichés
like, "If this weather's not your style,
    just stick around a little while."
Or, "The crops are being made."
    And yes, "It's ninety in the shade."
Poor old Rover lies and pants
    while the tree frog choir chants.
Little whirlwinds dance and play
    and you hear the old folks say,
"Don't see the wind stir up the sand."
    "Won't have no rain to cool the land."
"It ain't gonna rain no more, no more."
    "Young feller, that sun's what made me poor."
"Old man," I think, "you're still around,
    be glad God gave us this dusty ground."
Yes, summer's hot but it won't be long
    till Old Man Winter will come along.
You'll gripe and groan about the cold
    and we'll all listen because you're old.
But the summer's heat is fine with me,
    and ask the kids, they'll all agree
that summer is a lot more fun
    than getting all that homework done.

Getting A Rearing

By Equest'

Have you ever eaten tripe?
Or, have you ever hunted snipe?
The taste each leaves is much the same
and someone surely is to blame!

Has eggplant ever curled your lip?
Or, have you had to eat parsnip?
They both will turn your stomach, true;
But, at the table, what can you do?

Sauerkraut will rot your socks,
And Navy beans taste just like rocks;
But, when your dad says, "These you'll eat!"
You know you'll never leave your seat!

Visual Arts and Music

By: Equest'

Listen! Listen!
Look! Look!
Understand?
No!

Conglomerate pigments;
Personal interpretations;
Opinions, laughter,
Nothing definite,
Boredom infinite!
Why?

We're listening now —
To what?
More conglomerate.
Beautiful? Yes!
Meaning? Your own.
Mine?

Bach, Beethoven, Brahms;
All the rest
Make this course required.
    GRONK!

Author's note: This was written at JBU my freshman year. It was published in the campus newspaper, *The Threefold Advocate*.

The Senator

By: Equest'

The angry orb flings its piercing
  gaze across the room
    to search the souls of men
      whose gaze cannot
        return the glare.

The angry orb, razed by bits
  of hate, violence, tragedy,
    burns with a fire unquenchable
    because a death has forced it
    open for so long.

The angry orb scans the mob
  who caused its irritation
    and made its maps of red
    and scarlet deepen—
      deepen and burst
        into tears
          of passion.

The angry orb reflects the image
  of the past, reviewing deaths
    and wounds previously spent,
      anticipating cool relief
      of night.

The angry orb looks on and on,
  and sees in truth its night
    of healing sleep and rest
    will never come.

The angry orb of world, continent, country,
  state, county, city, family, individual —
    searches for solutions and asks the question,
      "Why?"

The Farmer

By: Equest'

Some people speak of the farmer
with a look of contempt in their eye;
they don't bother to think that without him
the country would wither and die.

The farmer's life span is shortened,
his back becomes permanently bent
from working from daylight to midnight
in order to just pay the rent.

His life is made up of heartbreak
when nature has taken his crop;
or the wind has shifted his seeding,
and the sky won't give up a drop.

A hail storm may ravage his wheat,
or blight may destroy his corn;
or rust may ruin his bean crop,
or his oats may be whipped by a storm.

Grasshoppers move in with their mandibles
and lay waste a field of good grain
while the frustrated farmer watches
and prays they return ne'er again.

A flood may wash away topsoil,
and erosion may claim a good field
that the farmer has plowed and harrowed
with dreams of success now concealed.

A 'dirt grubber' some folks may call him
as he stoops to break up a clod;
but, very few others will ever possess
a direct link like his with their God.

The man who never lives on a farm
may not understand the love
of the wind blowing free in his face,
or an unhampered view up above.

The same sun that causes the drought
wrinkles and toughens the skin
to prepare the farmer for winter,
with its cold, biting force of the wind.

You'll find it's very few farmers
who succumb to drugs or alcohol;
it's the farmer with tough, fibered morals
who stabilizes the wild, rocking world.

Without a country of farmers,
the cities would crumble and fold;
people would revert to the jungles,
and the earth would be covered with mold.

His job means more than just money,
it's a life of intangible reward;
it buys him the self-satisfaction
that most folks can never afford.

Spoiled Victor

By: Equest'

In bough and branch,
  leaf cover camouflage,
    crows nest lookout
      panorama, field
        and garden, food.

Sticks, yarn, twigs, bits,
  dedication, protection —
    breezy, lofty,
      peaceful,
        home.

Bright and dull plumage
  together work tirelessly,
    forgetting nothing;
      Nature's memory —
        Excitement! Excitement!
          Four speckled life bulbs!

Endless waiting, vigilant protection,
  Earth's horn of plenty —
    lawn, insects,
      garden hose,
        porch light —
          A crack!
            A peep!
              My fledglings,
                secure!

On the ground — a flicking tail,
  a single bound,
    bark aids claw,
      beak at eye,
        feather-cluttered paw —
          ravaged nest,
            murdered wife,
              appetite unslaked.

Victorious spoiler,
  uncaring criminal,
    wanton, blood-thirsty murderer;
      only bits of children left;
        little bodies ripped and broken.
          Oh, damn the law of nature!

Soul Exhumed
By: Equest'

How selfishly we stand
   at the grave
      of one loved.

For whom do we really care?
   For Body soon lowered away?
      Or someone else standing close by
         In bowel-torn grief?

Whose loss is whose gain?
   Unanswered questions flit by —
      disregarded.

Where has this life gone?
   To ashes or dust no spirit declines —
      so, why grieve?

It is Self ...
   for whom
      we weep.

Somnambulism Attempting

By: Equest'

A'drifting, drifting, drifting —
weightless go a'drifting;
through airy worlds of mist,
take yourself a'drifting.

A'drifting, drifting, drifting —
on nebulae of vapor misting,
slowly while away a day,
by going on a'drifting.

A'drifting, drifting, drifting —
past eons ahead or behind;
fly among the barriers of time,
as you take yourself a'drifting.

A'drifting, drifting, drifting —
to bottomless ocean depths,
or beyond this world's celestial sphere,
on lovely wings of drifting.

A'drifting, drifting, drifting —
farther from reality,
to memories of loves long lost,
because you were a'drifting.

A'drifting, drifting, drifting —
imaginings of evermore,
in darkness or in colors many,
will you still be a'drifting?

A'drifting, drifting, drifting —
tossing, turning, quietly yielding
to the creeping sensuality of sleep,
while you were a'drifting.

Sarcasm Or Sincerity?

By: Equest'

Emotions, feeling, intimate depth —
surfaced by listening;
music composed by classical greats
with lives devoted to human expression.

Only the masters achieve the climax —
the climax groped for by all humanity.
But it's ours, ours for the listening,
because the masters were good.

Russian Woman

By: Equest'

Flail, flail—damned accursed wheat!
Blow, blow! Oh, lifeless wind, clean this wheat!
Stalin die and leave us rags of communism—
no cars, no trucks, no combines of capitalism.

Our bones and muscles ache with strain,
from winnowing ancestors' ancient grain.
Our hearts and souls scream out, "Relief!"
"Give us, our God, a respite brief."

No freedom here, no peace on Earth.
What bastard dared to give me birth?
Blow through sick wind and clean the chaff,
drown out these peoples' hopeless laugh.

We hear so much we are to fear;
who knows what truth comes in my ear?
My roots are deep, my soul here lies,
I'll kill the capitalistic spies!

From "Freedom Land," the USA,
We hear so many things today:
"World peace, world peace," we hear them cry.
But, whose U2 fell from our sky?

What's that? It's quitting time so soon?
It hardly seems that long since noon.
The wheat is stored, there's no more sun,
I hope the children have the home chores done.

Random Imponderables

By: Equest'

So radiant, so alive!
It comes only from perception.
What is perception?
Seeking? Peering? Blinking?
Insight is that inward perception —
Insight into that held valuable.
Can human form avail such truth?
We look around us — only to see.
What do we see?
Only that for which we are looking!
We believe only what we wish to believe.
We see only as deeply as the pearlish hue which deceives.
But what is pure?
Only that which we recognize as purity.
We find this in love only—for nothing else can shape
    so staunch a core.
With respect, we admire;
    in love, we respect.
Oh lovers, where is y our admiration?
Oh love, where is your foundation?
        In God.

Paternal Concern

By: Equest'

I will build a house of mine —
  endeared — treasured —
    homing beacon, love laden,
      treasure stuffed,
        my children.

A house of mine —
  song-filled, uplifting,
    unity — resting place
      for weary feet;
        a gracious reigning queen.

House of mine —
  jewel bedecked,
    noise abounding,
      mussed and lived in,
        briny pillows,
          understanding.

My house —
  a shell,
    wood, sweat, stone;
      more than just a house —
        my home.

Mother's Face

By: Equest'

A four-lane, super, modern turnpike
   strikes its way across the face of
      Dear Old Mother Earth and leaves
         its eternal scar upon her precious
           cheek— oil-splattered,
             grease-spotted,
               glass-pitted, sunburned,
                  and pocked with white lines.

Knowing way leads on to way,
   the turnpike grudgingly makes its gradual
     condescension into the waiting
       mouth of yesterday's turnpike, now
         a contemptible two-lane wrinkle
           adding more lines to Mother's face —
             freckled from bloody wrecks,
              open sores of chuckholes,
                warts of asphalt pushed up
                  by pounding tires.

The two-lane highway soon reverts to
  nothing but a narrow, gravel road
    which boasts of choking dust
      so thick it blots the lights of cars
        and leaves this dandruff plague
          to dull the highlights of
            field and tree — Mother's ageless hair —
              eroded ditches,
                washboard surface
                    mud fingers wresting control
                  from the wheel.

Gravel road gives way to trail —
   Mother's only natural wrinkle —
     leading back to timeless years
       of man's unknowing distances
         traversed by unconcerned
           slashing, carving of a beautiful face;
             softened by a verdant, moist, pleasant
           fern and moss;
          flower-strewn,
            perfume of freshness
          on a simple
         path.

Inevitability

By: Equest'

Satisfaction, oh wondrous satisfaction!

A deed well done.

A love now won.

The season gone, the pennant won.

The games begin inside the gym.

The muscle aches, the casted breaks.

All trunks are gone, sweaters to don.

Grades to make, buses to take.

Leaves to rake, records to break.

Inside or outside; young man or old,

we all are affected

by the coming of cold...

        WEATHER.

The Gunnison

By: Equest'

Ever opening canyon doors,
    roaring over gorges' floors;
chewing, swallowing mud and sand,
    giving life to barren land.
Free rent I give to fish and fowl.
Sportsmen love my native growl.
Rangers bless my girth so wide
    when forest fires and I collide.
Parched lips and throats into me burst
    and suck my blood to quench their thirst.
If I weren't here, what would these do
    but wither and die in stagnant slough?
What are the cliffs without my breath
    but ears made deaf from the sound of death?
What gorge or canyon will deeper grow
    when dams have blocked my savage flow?
What man will come to tread the sod
    without a gun or fishing rod?
Where once did game and fish abound
    you'll hear the absence of my sound.
In place of my tranquility
    cities receive electricity.
The ugly sound of turbine hum
    will replace my musical kettle drum.
My voice is stilled, my life cut off,
    my timeless bed now just a trough.
Man will bring his big machine
    to rape this innocent defenseless queen.
He'll drill and grind and dig and blast,
    and I'll be losing the battle fast.
I'll fight like hell, you can count on me;
    but, I'm already whipped, it's reality.
And when they have their celebration,
    I will have one consolation —
They'll never know how dry I am
    until they've built that ugly dam!

The primary construction contract for the dam was awarded to the Tecon Corporation of Dallas, Texas, with notice to proceed on April 23, 1962. I wrote this poem when I heard all efforts to prevent construction had failed.

De Niggah

By: Equest'

Yo knows dat Ah'm 'merican;
yo knows dat Ah'm a man;
yo knows dat Ah got feelin's
e'vn tho' Ah'm black as Ah am.

Yo knows de her'tij Ah claim;
it's yo's 'n mahn — bof de same.
Yo wuz heah fust 'n dat Ah 'dmits;
but, yo brung me, is Ah t' blame?

Ah'm an ol' niggah nam'd Jed,
wuth nuffin' no mo' t' de worl';
'tahms Ah wisht Ah wuz de'd,
w'en 'nsults at me 'r hurl'd.

De Lo'd don' make no 'stinction
twixt yo 'n me 'n othus;
but, yo? Yo'd put me t' 'xtinction,
St'd o' bein' 'merican brothus.

Ah knows dat Ah'm blak 'n yo's w'ite;
but, Ah knows whut's 'rong 'n whut's raht.
Ah knows dat Ah need t' 'mprove;
Jist don' try t' push me, Ah'll move.

Ah don' wan' nun o' you char'ty,
'n Ah don' wan' yo money o' clo's;
jis' lemme 'lone 'n Ah'll git 'long,
a walk'n d' ro'd dat Ah choz.

Yo w'tes uv b'km awf'l smaht;
yo'v leahn'd how t' fi'te 'n mak' money;
but, de's wun t'ing dat yo've all f'got,
An dat's whut yo calls sy'kolgy.

Go hi'ah yo p'licemen 'n dogs 'n such truk;
yo'll fin' it'll be m'ty hahd
t' nok down 'n stomp on a bu'k
who'll dar' t' put up 'is g'ard.

Ah lay we ne'd mo' uner'stan'n —
yo, mah w'ite na'br 'n me —
'cause den der wudn' be no mo' brand'n
o' fi't'n, o' kil'n o' God's c'mpny!

Tahms Ah don' no mah o'n fo'ks,
wy, de way dy car'y on so;
dey aks lak w'eels wido't spokes,
a weav'n 'n woblin' wid no place t' go.

Ah don' stik up fo' de bla'ks;
Ah don' stik up fo' de w'ites;
Ah ain' stik'n up fo' no 'rongs;
Ahm jis' sti'k'n up fo de ri'tes.

Fi't'n 'n bleed'n 'n kil'n
do'n' git a body no whah;
but, luv'n 'n help'n 'n chil'un,
reac's on pe'p'l dat cah!

At Knighting

By: Equest'

What greater tribute can be said than,
"This man is pure?"

Can strength shadow purity?
Is courage valued more?

How noble stands a man of purity.
Purity has no sham or lie.
No enemy dare deny
      purity.

How just is one to question purity —
— foundation below the iron of love —
— gem of tempered steel?

The oyster's child, a pearl of purified sand —
— a lump of blackened charcoal —
— pressed and squeezed —
— to pure and matchless diamond.

These and man of
      purity.

Today's Tomorrow
By Equest'

Beginning life in alpine snow,
        a slim, silvery trickle,
gurgles, squirms and kicks its way
        Into forceful rivulet —
squeaking, crying, screaming —
        rocky cradle ...
igneous, metamorphic, sedimentary ...
trees (live and dead) ... forcing, winding
        pattern
against its natural will.

Focused notice
        of this babbling brook ...
maturing mainstream conquering
        boulders, trees
ordering prior course —
        now giving way.

Bearing sands and silt —
        societies' pollutants —
stream invades lowland — civilization —
        deposits Nature's by-product —
            vomits
into roaring rivers bearing barges
        strewing man across the land
in dirty irrigation ditches.

Salty grave, abyssal plain, sucks out the life;
        snowdrift womb melted — gone —
another cloud ...
        begins to snow.

Depression Destroyed: Optimism Qualified

A reading performed at John Brown University; American Heritage Seminar, 1965; by Equest'.

I am an individual.

I think. I trust. I hope. I have my faith.

I love. I'm strong. I'm weak. I'm brave.

And, I am afraid!

I hear the question: "Where is your Miami?" and I panic at my loss.

My faith in the American philosophy as a nation is gone and my mind is in a tumult seeking an answer to, "Where is your Miami?"

I have no Miami except an oasis of political representatives and these are rapidly evaporating and becoming more grains of sand to be carried away and relocated by the barren desert winds. I have been taught to cherish and revere my country — to unselfishly sacrifice my life unhesitatingly to protect my loves and United States.

The words of Patrick Henry haunt my soul and my nights are full of death with no liberty because my contemporary college peers have succumbed to rationalization. Their greed, ignorance, openly flouted rebellion against protecting my dreams and confidences is destroying me!

Is it destroying you?

My secure feelings fly from me each time I hear the stillness broken by the eerie siren that could be screaming, "AIR RAID! AIR RAID! AIR RAID!"

My country is no longer a haven of liberty, a bosom of peace, a land of Pilgrim's pride. I see it as a retarded child helplessly shackled by the chains of crime and corruption, terror and confusion and a land of prevaricating politicians.

My country, once thought of as the melting pot of the world, has turned its delicious harmony into a boiling turmoil of discrimination and stupid feuds between a black American and a white American instead of joining hands in an attempt to cooperate and rationally find solutions to problems that can't be legislated.

Even the children of America are no longer taught the real meaning of "I pledge allegiance;" rather, it has become merely a traditional ceremony to be tolerated and reserved for mockery in later years.

I cherish my flag and its symbols that penetrate deeper than the materialistic philosophy and so-called *'logic of tangibles'* that protect the draft card burner and communist sympathizers.

All these things, and many more, invade my thoughts and emotion centers. They stimulate my adrenals and threaten to drown the optimism which is my pedigree.

And then — and then — I remember, I AM AN AMERICAN!

I stem the flood of over-excitement with its gut-wrenching terror and pessimism.

I allow the faint flickering flame to expand and fill my frame with a bonfire of dedication and determination to rally around our flag with my many contemporaries who also are aware of the ever increasing problems of our nation yet don't give way to the depressions of a seemingly inevitable destruction.

My faith is renewed and I join the sparrow who mounted the eagle and flew higher than all the rest to become the champion.

I recognize the thousands, even millions, who, like myself, are pouring their souls into maintaining our nation and I know that many sparrows will not lose.

Our men in Korea, our men in Berlin, and now, our men in Vietnam, know the reasons for their duties and are suffering and dying for them — for us — the sparrows who care and will win, not the vultures who glean only the left-overs from the harvest!

> America, all hail!
>
> Though the foe within you set;
>
> You, the nation, shall prevail,
>
> For you're the greatest nation yet!

SECTION II

GOD IN MIND

New Life In A Scrub Oak

By: Equest'

A small scrub oak grew by my door
and I watched each year this battle;
the winds would howl, the snow would fly,
my, how those leaves did rattle.

Into the wind their backs they'd turn
to wage a defensive war;
courageous and strong, tenaciously cling
to branches with fibrous core.

I watched each day and some gave way
to Autumn's cooling air;
but, some held on in open defiance
not seeming even to care.

When winter came, the scrub oak fought
the ice and snowy flake.
Each leaf held on to his own branch
refusing his hold to break.

And, by the time spring rolled around,
the leaves had won again.
It seemed no summer breeze or rain
could ever hope to win.

Then one day, to my surprise,
the oak stood stripped and bare.
There at its feet I saw the leaves
gazing up in shocked despair.

A closer scrutiny then disclosed
the reason for their plight.
The winter with its storms had failed
but something else had done it right.

A look of peace and serenity
replaced the previous face.
New Life crept in, transformed the soul,
a change had taken place.

I knew a man some years ago
whom I shall call Scrub Oak.
And, like the leaves, his sins held on
in spite of all who spoke.

He fought the seasons' storms and winds
with all their preaching force;
and, though a few brown leaves fell off,
no wind could change his course.

Then one day, to his surprise,
a south wind touched his heart.
His roots were warmed, New Life crept in,
a change began to start.

First one brown leaf fell at his feet,
followed quickly by the rest.
His posture changed, he stood erect,
his face looked so refreshed.

Many storms have come and gone
and caused some green to fade;
But, New Life dwells too deep inside,
that's where the change was made.

Letter to Dr. J Vernon McGhee - 1968

1340 N. Main
Wheaton, IL 60189

27 October, 1968

Dear Dr. McGhee,

Several years ago, during one of y our annual visits to the campus of John Brown University, your message drew an analogy between a scrub oak tree and a Christian. At that time, there was a small scrub oak growing by the drive-way of our duplex and the analogy and association made such an impression that, every time I hear the leaves rattle in a big wind, I am reminded of it.

Today, here in Wheaton, we are having quite a wind storm and the leaves are blowing and rattling through the streets and I was inspired to write this poem. Although it isn't much as poetry, I hope you enjoy reading it.

Allow me this opportunity to express the admiration I have held for you, your dedication and the way you spoke to me each time it was my privilege to sit under your ministry.

My name is Lee Horsman (Equest' is my *nom de plume*) and I had the pleasure of taking part in three of your services at the Church of the Open Door when, as a member of the JBU Choir and Harmonaires, we visited Southern California.

Your daughter, Linda, is a great friend and classmate here at JBU.

I hope you enjoy this little effort at expressing a very fond memory.

Yours truly,

Lee Horsman

Why War, God?

By: Equest'

What kind of god would preordain
the storms of human suffering;
their wars and plagues and pestilence bear,
before the gentleness of the rain?

We cannot win with might or main
a peaceful life, no threat to bear,
unless somehow we first have fought
a war or tyrant's sword of pain.

Somehow it seems we never gain
our goal of peace for all mankind;
for somewhere, someone always cries
unjustly crushed with cruel disdain.

Does man enjoy the conquering strain
belonging to those warriors bold?
Does glory, booty, pride or greed
satisfy the conqueror's brain?

Black, Jew, Indian strain
for justice, peace, equality;
and in their quest for centuries
still daily share a bloody stain.

The fiddler on his roof still stands.
The black still looks for equal rights.
The Red Man bucks his harness reins.
Our pride won't let us join hands.

And who can justify one bomb?
Does might make right?
Can treaty or ally demand
we rip a baby from its womb?

What is this thirst that drives men on,
to kill and maim with war machines?
Can government of any sort
demand we fight till we're all gone?

The simple brotherhood of man
demands an equal place for all;
a place to live and laugh and love —
return to where it all began.

Must peace and simple joys of life
be bought with pain and suffering?
The histories of mankind seem filled
with these things bought with blood and strife.

Is this God's basic human law?
Or will He give us ample time
to cure this ageless paradox,
and, somehow, mend so great a flaw?

Every day our prayer must be
to end all war and suffering;
to spread abroad a peaceful quest —
give every man equality.

Man alone creates all wars,
and he alone decides their course;
and he alone must stop this game,
that everyone on earth abhors.

Upon Acceptance

By: Equest'

When life was full of bitterness,
He changed it all to tenderness —
what can I do but love Him?

He took my hand and led me up a road,
a road He walked so long ago
to end His day with no one there
to share with Him His tears and broken heart —
What can I do but love Him?

The world is full of winter with chilling cold and,
"I don't care...," of heart.
This season's winds with icy blades
preserves the hate in peoples' souls,
but, this can change with warming rays
brought into life as I have found.
What can I do but love Him?

What can I do but love Him
when I feel His warmth force me to say,
"I love you," to a dirty little boy way down in Harlem?

Can anyone resist his soul
when something there
will make him care
about a friend who has a friend that's died?

If life is filled with dark despair
and you can't say, "I love you,"
to a world that needs your love,
then open up your heart and you will find
that you can't help but love Him.

Summer Sanctuary

By: Equest'

A holy and hallowed place
   beckons my heart to attend
      its service of quiet tranquility
         to worship in peace and serenity.

It's a cathedral of calm solitude
   where I visit only with thoughts of my heart
      and, alone in serene quietude,
         the Spirit of God whispers my name.

My holy and hallowed retreat
   is but an old, dry, washed-out gully
      where flash floods have carved their names
         in the sand of a dry, desolate prairie.

I watch as desert creatures stalk their prey
   along the shadowed walls of to them such a gorge,
      and I feel the coolness of the shadow
         fight its war against the
            creeping, seeping desert heat.

My thoughts and meditations seem to be so infinite;
   and yet, I feel the oppressive weight
      of an unfulfilled and hollow life
         without a way to serve mankind.

I pray, "Oh God, give me a way
   to serve You best by helping man;
      please take my life but give me peace
         through knowing I have done my best.

"What can I do? Where can I go?
   Who can I meet to rid my soul
      of hollow, purposeless living
         in a world of need and depravity?"

A scorpion works his way along the shale and clay
   to seek a meal of unsuspecting creature.
      He sends his streaking, fiery pain to end
         the life of spider, bug or locust.

The purple shadow of a passing cloud
   brings brief relief to a scorched earth
      and lends its refreshment to those below
         whose thorn and needle are brittle baked.

My reverie returns from these brief interruptions:
   what were my thoughts before?
      Oh yes, a life wasted by subsistence existence
         with no spiritual fulfillment.

A cricket chirps his cheery music while
   a grasshopper buzzes overhead
      and a hawk circles lazily on a draft
         and a lonely wasp, unhampered, passes.

My God! Where did that snake come from?
   The rattler stalks an unwary mouse asleep
      In the shady overhang — but now asleep forever
         in the prairie king's constricting coil.

The eternal struggle for life goes on
   among the weak as well as for the strong.
      But fiercer battles rage within the soul
         of man whose enemy is his Self.

Self marks the difference between
   the man and hawk or wasp or mouse;
      and yet, who is the stronger?
         I fear the man is not
            whose Self he cannot conquer.

The sand strewn floor on which I lie
   and ponder all these things
      will never know a battle
         of a soul like mine;
            but, only lies in wait for man
               to come and rest here.

This floor will know no broom except
   the wind or rushing stream;
      and yet, its cleanliness far exceeds
         the sin and filth of human heart.

A western sky with mountain line
   glows with radiance from the Master painter's
      brilliant strokes and says
         it's time for me to
            make my way
               homeward.

I Heard God

By: Equest'

I heard God's voice in a waterfall
   as I listened intently there.
I heard Him whisper in my ear,
   asking for my prayer.

My earnest prayer, oh precious Lord?
   Let someone hear your call
who's never heard the voice of God
   as from a waterfall.

Speak to me, and others too,
   as from a waterfall.
What would you have your servants do?
   Please, let us hear your call.

I felt His moist fingertips,
   as the spray caressed my face.
I felt the precious tenderness
   of God's instilled embrace.

Please touch another lonely heart,
   who hasn't felt the spray —
a golden matchless gift impart
   to guide him on his way.

The streaks of Jesus' dying tears
   were mirrored in the foam.
I stood and gazed with brimming eyes,
   thinking, "Jesus died alone."

God's Choicest

By: Equest'

Grind away at granite bluff,
   sift my grit through any stuff;
nothing can against me stand
   for I'm a tiny grain of sand.

I hoe the soil, I smooth the stone,
   the world is mine, by wind I'm blown.
My friends and I can blot the sun
   or stem the mightiest river's run.

No one I know dares me defy,
   I am the land, I rule the sky.
Man will surely get here soon,
   but, I'm here first, for I'm the moon.

At man's puny effort to keep me out,
   I take my time and win the bout.
His glass and doors are funnier still
   that's me — right there — on the window sill!

Deep down here they'll soon explore,
   but, I make up the ocean floor.
I'm carried along by current and swirl,
   I'm even the center of every pearl.

I have no fear of war or bomb
   I line the walls of every tomb.
When God created this bit of land,
   He used me first, His grain of sand.

All For What?

By: Equest'

The Rose of Heaven wilted down
   and dropped to earth its petals
      one by one.

Each petal bore the sweetest fragrance
   of the Maker's hands —
      the precious sweat of Love.

One petal fell and said, "I Am."
   "I'm here for all to see, to hear,
      to follow or to cast aside."

Another, Love, drifted down
   and felt the crushing stamp
      of human feet defile its perfection.

With salty dewdrops from Love's eyes,
   He healed the blind and prayed
      for those who mocked His touch.

When Peace came down and found His place
   in hearts that never knew before the gift,
      He left a seed of procreation.

The petal, though, in human form,
   came strong and brave, met heartbreak,
      pain and Love betrayed.

He bore the dust, sun, wind and rain,
   the hate, loneliness, mockery —
      and, in return, gave hope.

God gave His son, the best He had,
   to carry the cross, suffer the lash,
      submit to the rusty spike.

All He had for contemptible man —
   and, from the cross, with side spear riven —
      His eyes plead: "Christian, what have you given?"

A Poem For Dr. Oiesen

By: Equest'

No art form stirs
   the human soul
like melodies intensely
      sung
   or rhythms ... chanted ...
from the loft,
     or harmonies — pianissimo —
                      soft.

World's of music lost
     in time
   pre-date man's history ...
parchment scroll.
     A bard recounts
   the trials of men
in music that defies the ...
                      pen.

The great king, Saul,
   wracked with pain,
called for David's
   voice and harp.
A shepherd's
   voice and instrument
brought comfort to this king's
                      torment.

Since God created angels' voices
          MUSIC
has inspired mankind;
   heralding the Savior's birth,
bringing Heaven's touch to
                      Earth.

Though many masters
   with their scores
have stood the test of time on earth,
            choirs
of Heaven strike their chord
   and harmonize to praise the
                      Lord.

... poem to Dr. Oiesen continued....

How many lives
    your hands have touched
in graceful, sweeping arcs of
            LOVE;
countless concerts,
Cathedral Choirs, the
            GIFT
    you've given still....
                          Inspires.

In vain we try
    to say to you
how much you've meant
    to all of us.
You've helped so many of us
           Grow,
      THANK Y OU
so much...
                         Dr. "O!"

1325 Sylvan
Plano, TX 75074

11 March, 1974

Dr. Mabel Oiesen
John Brown University
Siloam Springs, AR 72761

Dear Dr. Oiesen,

It was the fall of 1962 when, as a freshman, I 'made the choir.' I'll tell you what it meant to me — in four years on College Hill, I never once missed a rehearsal or performance.

Do you remember the production of Oklahoma? It was, undoubtedly, the highlight of my life up to that time. I'll never forget the beautiful black light scene created by you and Dr. Woodland, nor the trials of poor Mr. Murphy transposing, re-transposing and sweating in the 'pit.'

The spring tour that year took us to Chicago, Buffalo and into Canada where we did a high school assembly and you quickly changed the entire program to *a cappello* because, as you put it, "— that piano sounds like a bird is strangling in it!"

That was the first of four tours I was privileged to make. Just for old times' sake, allow me to review a few of the more memorable episodes.

We were in a church somewhere in California when a stray cat sauntered down the center aisle and created such a ruckus the entire congregation and choir had a knee-slappin' laugh.

While we were still in California, prior to a Sunday morning service, Bill Hartman and I went water skiing with our host and barely made it to the church in time to don our robes! That same tour took us through a blinding sand storm near Spearman, Texas.

Thanks to you, those are great memorable moments for a young impressionable college student. Yet, as great as they are, it was the Harmonaire experience I count as the highlight of my college life.

I realize that all these experiences would never have been if you had not taken the interest in me that you did. It is impossible to express my gratitude and appreciation for everything you have done and all you have meant to me.

I could continue this, recalling incident after incident, personality after personality, from the private voice lessons to Visual Arts and Music; from practice room to recital (who will ever forget Dave Mallory's "— aw, forget it!"), countless choir rehearsals, musical productions, and so forth, but, I won't.

In closing, I will cite two things that, though I may live a hundred years, I will never forget:

- During a choir rehearsal my freshman year, you suddenly stopped everything and stared right at me. I could not imagine what you thought I had done. As I recall, we were rehearsing on the risers. Without a word, you made your way through the first two rows to the tenor section, you grabbed my face and kissed me — full on the mouth! When all the hysteria had died down, you explained that you had always wanted to kiss a man with a mustache. My mustache was terribly sparse and anemic. To this day, I can't grow a thick one; however, if I thought it would get you to kiss me, I'm sure I could give it a try.
- The second reflection I would like to attend is that which I am sure will be mentioned in every letter you receive from this solicitation. If ever a life has been lived that epitomizes the message of what must be regarded as the eternal theme song of the JBU Cathedral Choir, it must be that of Dr. Oiesen. It is my sincerest hope that, as you look back through the years, you will see many of us who are living better and loving stronger because we had the privilege of the example of your life and, together, we can all truly sing, "A Mighty Fortress Is Our God!"

May God bless you,

Leroy R. Horsman

This letter attended the poem to be included in a collection solicited by JBU for the retirement celebration of Dr. Oiesen. All letters were bound into a leather dossier and I was told, several years later, that Dr. O read my poem and this letter often enough that the dossier fell open to this letter and that the pages are stained with her tears.

Section III

SONGS

A Touch Of Tenderness

By: Equest'

What goes beyond the threat of war,
    and bridges seas from shore to shore,
and lifts us up to heaven's door?
    A touch of tenderness.

This root of love compels us all
    to bend our knees and hear the call
of brotherhood afraid to fall
    and needs some tenderness.

        What Mommy does when Baby starts to cry;
        and what God did to light the midnight sky;
        then, why oh why, do we refuse to try
        a touch of tenderness?
        As morning sun lifts off the sparkling dew
        and bathes the world in rainbows' vivid hue,
        then, why don't you do all that you can do?
        Try using tenderness.

A mother's son sent off to fight,
    it matters not which side is right;
he could be killed just out of sight
    of Mother's tenderness.

The ghetto streets so filled with need
    look out with tear-filled eyes that plead,
"Is no one there whose heart will heed,
    our cries for tenderness?"

A red man cried at Wounded Knee,
    frustration filled with agony,
while soldiers danced in victory,
    where was their tenderness?

A yellow child cries out in fear,
    "America, why are you here?"
The bombs explode, he'll never hear,
"This is our tenderness!"

Author's note: The original melody has never been scored.

Stillborn

By: Equest'

The day I was born, I heard the wind call:
"Come to the mountains where the pines grow tall.
Come to the prairie where your soul blows free,
and the shifting, whispering sands are me."

My cradle still stands empty down in Tennessee.
My father takes my mother to the cemetery.
Feel my touch, hear my cry, as you see the trees bend,
be glad your son was chosen as a brother of the wind.

As an active young man, you'll watch me grow strong,
as the spring and summer rains sing my song.
And, by autumn, I'll have the voice of a man;
the leaves will leave their trees at my command.

As the years roll by, your son will grow old;
you'll feel his manly strength in the Norther's chilling cold;
another baby cries down in Tennessee,
but, his cradle now is empty —
he has left to follow me.

Have You Listened?

By: Equest'

Have you listened to the Savior lately?
    Have you tuned your ear to hear His voice?
He will help you make the right decision;
    ask the Holy Spirit for His choice.

        He knows the burden that you bear;
        He wants to share your every care;
        If you will only go to Him in prayer;
        Have you listened to His tender pleading?
        Listen while the Spirit speaks to you.

Are you walking close beside Him daily?
    Do you find companionship with Him?
Do you talk with Him as if He's present?
    Is He the one you call your dearest friend?

Repeat chorus.

There are two melodies for this song: 1) my original and 2) a better one by Jerri Ericson Turner — neither has been scored and both will be lost when I'm no longer around to sing them.

Abandoned

By: Equest'

It's a rip off world
   with a rip off God,
and a rip off life
   full of plastic hopes
      and fears.
And it's easy
   to condemn your soul
with a shotgun wedding
   or a bottle full
      of tears.

      Go ahead and have your baby anyway,
      he told you he'd be coming back any day;
      afraid of what your folks or friends may have to say,
      you know they'll take your baby if you run away.

It's a rip off world
   with a rip off God,
and a rip off life
   full of plastic hopes
      and fears.
And it's easy
   to condemn your soul
with a shotgun wedding
   or a bottle full
      of tears.

      A lonely teenage girl with a lover who's gone,
      and left her with a problem to face all alone;
      getting high in dirty alleys is her only escape
      from thinking of that lover she's been tryin' to hate.

It's a rip off world
   with a rip off God,
and a rip off life
   full of plastic hopes
      and fears.
And it's easy
   to condemn your soul
with a shotgun wedding
   or a bottle full
      of tears.

Sandy Sea

By: Equest'

Moon shines bright on prairie silent;
stars gaze down — no noise at all;
cattle dozin', it's so quiet —
all you hear is the coyote's call.

Across the sand, night winds blowin',
free and light, blowin' too slow;
always movin', where's it goin'?
someone said it's blowin' down to Mexico.

Cricket chirps, dawn's awakenin',
locust buzz, vipers uncoil;
sun comes up, starts a'bakin';
soon the man appears for a day of toil.

Upturned earth dries in clods;
kangaroo mice seek new homes;
devil horns crack their seed-filled pods;
deer flies swarm where the antelope roams.

Do You Believe?
By: Equest'

Why do things happen
      that we don't understand?
Why do we let things
      get out of hand?
What forces are these
      that cast us about,
grabbing our minds,
      leaving us all in doubt?
I don't have the answers,
      but I know One who does,
He created the world
      and He cares about us.

      Do you believe?
      Do you believe?
      Do you believe
      He watches over you and me?
      His eyes perceive what we can't see.
      Allow His love to set you free.
      Live out this life in liberty.

What makes us fight wars
      when nobody wins?
What makes us kill brothers
      that could have been friends?
For God, home and country
      the war cry rings out!
Where once it was so,
      I now have my doubt.
I don't have the answers,
      but I know One who does,
He created the world
      and He cares about us!

Cast Your Bread Upon The Water

By: Equest'

Does your life seem unfulfilling?
Can't you find someone who's willing
      to share the world instilling
            all your love;
            all your love.
Oh, my brother, in pain and sorrow,
walk with me until tomorrow;
till there's no need to borrow,
from a friend, from a friend.

Just cast your bread upon the water,
      soul of the deep will eat your bread.
Spirit moves and you don't see him,
      but He moves inside your head!
Black mass grips at your emotions,
      canine blood runs down your chest!
You wrestle with a naked body
      on an altar meant for love.
Don't give in, he'll take your body;
      like a toy, he'll wind you up!
You'll cry out for exorcism,
      "Oh, my God, please lift me up!"
And up you will be lifted,
      the Son of God has heard your cry!
You cast your bread upon the water,
      went through hell to find your way;
Now you're high on something greater,
      Loving Him from day to day!
Loving Him from day to day!

A Cowboy Falls

By: Equest'

I met my handsome cowboy
  at the Denver Livestock Show.
He won my heart in just the way
  he won the rodeo.
He asked me if I'd marry him
  and share a cowboy's life;
the greatest times I ever had
  were as that cowboy's wife.

      But now my tears would fill the bottle
        you left empty on the bar.
      I cry myself to sleep each night,
        just wondering where you are.
      Oh, the story's told so often
        and you know it has no end;
      won't you please forget your whiskey,
        and think of me again?

His dream was just to ride in all
  the big time rodeos.
Together we took part in all
  the major western shows.
We never talked about the time
  he'd take his final ride;
I never said a word to him,
  just kept my fears inside.

That final ride came all too soon,
  he broke his back in two.
And when the cheering crowds are gone,
  what does a cowboy do?
One drink was all he took at first
  to help him fight the pain;
but now that whiskey's killing him,
  and driving me insane!

Section IV

Limited Distribution

Passions Expressed While Listening to a Piano Concert on a Stereo Record

By: Equest'

Gripped by pulsating, insatiable desires to free my soul — myself — in a liberating denial of any suppression. I feel my being aching, torturously straining against society that denies me the freedom of shouting — inability to voice my tremors in music, music, music, music, music!

Give me music — a Williams on the piano to express my driving passions that threaten to make my peers call me mad.

Oh how I'd love to throw up my arms, lift my face heavenward and allow my pent up spirit to gush forth from a heretofore mute mouth. Oh God, let me be free — free to release my entire being into effortless song — natural music issuing from a desolate desert fenced by mountains of society's classifications of a man's personality.

Is it conceit, egotism, pride, or selfishness to allow one's self to liberate his soul in singing?

Let them all listen and be damned!

I don't care anymore and the chains of institution bind me no more.

More! More! More ... more bass, more treble ...

JUST GIVE ME VOLUME!

But, now, now this wild outburst of passion has subsided.

David has played his harp and the Saul in my soul has retired to await another awakening when the pacifism has lost its keen edge and my enslaved emotions shall again rebel and strain once again against the chains of society, classification and personal misconceptions — for — ...

....I am defeated again...

> Script for a one actress, one act short stage play.

Soul Of A Child

By: Equest'

Will I ever be able to purify myself again?

My old man's grubby paws pushing me into his "— well prepared" bomb shelter.

I still get the creeps thinking of his clammy hands shoving me into this cubicle — black museum of daily horrors.

Mom, sis, the old man and me — God, I'm a woman, seventeen. Brought down like a mole to live in a worm's house for only God knows how long by a shrieking siren.

My soul laughs in derision at my old man — big exec' before, but now a sweaty, grizzled papa mole wearing his grimy white shirt, crooked tie and taking such care of his 'gator hide, buckled shoes. He makes me sick.

I'm not impressed with all his exaggerated explanations of radiation and all this jazz about rationing facilities to get us by till — how long did he say?

Just like him; finally says something I want to hear then won't repeat it.

Who the hell cares anyway? I'll leave this hole tomorrow by myself if I damn well please.

Now, where's the john? Oh God, you gotta be kiddin' — the chemical mess behind that curtain? Forget it! I can hold it till hell freezes over before I'll publicize my privates to that old bastard.

How long we been here? Something's wrong with your dial. Two hours your ass. I know we've been here five hours anyway.

God, what a thing to have to give in to — letting my old man get his kicks listening to me urinate behind this curtain with my toes poking out.

Mom, mom, wise up! Can't you see he's overemphasizing this nuclear holocaust? It's a build-up to satisfy his ego. This shelter was his security substitute and now he's using a simple test to make us his dependents. He's Neanderthal.

No, I don't want to join your bridge game. Play strip poker if you want — nothing's private anymore anyway.

I'm hungry but damned if I'll eat that dehydrated crap in those dusty boxes. They can have them. I'll wait till tomorrow and raid the 'fridge in the house.

It must be seven or eight by now — damn, Eric was to pick me up at 7:30 and we were going to see *Failsafe* before we found our parking place and really entertained ourselves; first the pot then — God he's got a groovy body. Damn it; my old man's making me miss all that. This cot isn't too bad if Eric was here.

O.K., give me one of those crummy cookies so full of vitamins and all that crap.

Why can't I wash my hands?

Water rations your ass — O.K., I'll join your primate family till you get over your game.

A week? We're not staying in this hole a week! Mom, get him off it. I'll die in two more hours at this rate.

Oh no, what a time to start my period. I've kept it a secret from my old man for four years and now he'll know. God, I'll die.

What's this medieval napkin dispenser? Mom, I don't use these things. God, what do I do now? I'm becoming middle class.

What's the sweat? I'm just leaving. Don't bug me, old man!

What radiation? You're cracked!

Ow! Ow! I can't believe you slapped me!

If Eric knew, he'd kill you! No, no, don't hit me again!

Two, three, four days...

Stagnate water, foul air from my old man's rotten intestines... everybody but me with bad breath 'cause my old man, Strangelove, in his preparations, forgot mouthwash and won't allow us water enough to brush our teeth.

... continued

I'll have him institutionalized as soon as we get out of here. Mom too, maybe. Anyway, she's not playing the role. Maybe it's a conspiracy to get me just because I've been ahead of them so long.

He says we can leave in three more days. We'll see what happens then.

God I'm dirty. If Eric or the neighbors are waiting for us to emerge, I'll kill myself.

He can't keep me from using the water the night before to set my hair and clean up.

Maybe I'll go out naked and claim he was using me. They'd put him away for sure then.

Five days, six — tomorrow he says we can look out — God, what an egotist. Why can't I use the water for my hair?

You hate me!

Open the damn door!

I expected the cool fresh air. I was dying to see the house, yard, street, pool full of friends and, surprisingly, a blue sky with the bright sun broken by the big shade trees I used to climb.

Oh, God!

What is this?

Nothing but black dust raining from a dull gray sky piling up in incendiary drifts...

...Daddy! Daddy! Daddy!

My Trip

By: Equest'

Luxury — deep in misty hills
  and vales of luxury — fragrant
    mounds of white whipped cream
    and fleecy clouds to roll in.

Unbounded, bottomless pit of savory
  smells and mists to tickle my
    naked parts and make me
      tingle with pure expression
        of myself without a chain
          of *more* — guiltless.

To bask in heavenly passion
  pouring from my soul
    because my lips —
      my fingertips —
        have been caressed
          by darting streaks
            of lightning.

Enfolded in the weightless fog of ecstasy,
  freedom in kaleidoscopic mists of
    vague and shapeless hues and
      shades of forms I've never seen
      I feel the spasms
        wanting only more.

My cloud is drifting, blown asunder
  by winds of social force —
    my liberating aversions gone
      only to return
        by losing face with people
          when I take
            my trip.

Spicy

By: Equest'

Since variety is the spice of life,
Repeat this poem to your wife:
If the plural for mouse is mice;
Then, the plural for spouse,
Must be spice.

I Love My Pharmacy

By: Equest'

The touching of some furry stuff
  Is touching — yet, is touching not.
    I feel its presence soft and tingly
      and let excitement surge
        within me.
The passion swells within my soul
  and tickles like an oozing mud
    between my toes
      or like the moist caress of sweating palm
        or firm bite of pliant flesh
        between my teeth.
It's working magic now —
  this lump of crystal cube
    and myriads flash
      in frenzied, flashing paths
        and patterns
          through lenses dilated
            to let my self
              pass through.
I feel the glorious heat seep upward
  From my toe-tips and explode
    In orbs made raw by bright
      and vivid bursts of luminescence,
        color schemes no eye but mine
          has ever captured,
            yet, no canvas, film or palette
            can hold it.
Again, and again, and again —
  let me feel and know this tension —
    with a hurt that feels so good —
      a masochistic plea to sweat
        and strain and feel another
          do the same
            with imprisoned passion
              finding satisfaction.

END

About The Author

Lee (Leroy), son of Wilbur & Irene Horsman, was born in Memphis, TN, in 1944. After a brief stop in Des Moines, IA, at age three he began life with his family in Boone, CO, where he resided till his high school graduation. Following graduation, he enrolled in John Brown University in Siloam Springs, AR. Following his graduation in 1967, he accepted a public school teaching position in Wheaton, Il. Deciding to leave teaching, he relocated his family to Dallas, TX, where he lived twenty-two years before relocating to California. His career in sales included positions in the Bay Area, Fresno and San Diego. From San Diego, he relocated to Chicago, then to Indiana and Maine. He moved to Colorado Springs where he retired from a long career in wireless communications sales.

The poems, songs and prose contained in this collection represent a lifetime of writing intended to express his interest in recording his contemplations on life. From his first poem, *The Gunnison*, written in 1962, Lee's inspiration to write has kept him actively writing to the present day. In 2003, he self-published his first novel, *Jew, Christian, MUSLIM, WAR!*, followed by *Stemming The Tide*, *Prairie Boy (autobiography)*, his second novel, *Rocking The Cradle (Of Civilization)*-first in a series he calls: *The Second Greatest Story Ever Told*, and *Contemplations*.

Made in the USA
San Bernardino, CA
20 April 2017